Surviving Nature's Fury

Surviving Nature's Fury

 A catalogue record for this book is available from the National Library of Australia

Cover Design: Karen L Feldbauer
Cover Image: Photo taken and edited by Karen L Feldbauer
Images: All images taken by Karen L Feldbauer have been remastered from old kodak photos using Expert RAW and Adobe Photoshop . The photo of Faye Feldbauer is an old portrait taken in her early twenties and therefore photographer is unknown. The VW photos was printed from the internet and remastered using Adobe Photoshop and is only used as a reference as I have no photos of mum's VW Beetle.

Also available as an e-book

Copyright © 2025 by Karen L Feldbauer
Publisher: Pure Heart Publishing
All rights reserved. No part of this book may be reproduced in any manner whatsoever without written permission except in the case of brief quotations embodied in critical articles and reviews.
First Printing, 2025

This book is dedicated to my mother, Faye whose bravery on that January day in 1969 saved our lives during the bush fires. Her courage and instinctive strength remain a guiding light in my life.

To my father, Alby, who taught me the value of hard work, resourcefulness, and practical skills that gave me the confidence to face whatever challenges came my way.

To my siblings, children, and dear friends thank you for the love, patience, and laughter that carried me through the hardest of times and reminded me that joy can always be found, even in the aftermath of disaster.

And finally, to every Australian who has endured the fury of nature whether through fire, flood, cyclone, or storm. May these stories remind you that you are not alone, that resilience grows in community, and that courage often reveals itself in the most unexpected moments.

CONTENTS

SURVIVING NATURE'S FURY		ii
DEDICATION		iv
PREFACE		vii
INTRODUCTION		ix
TIMELINE		xi

1	1969 Bushfire	1
2	1969 My Bushfire Story	6
3	After the Fire	10
4	1969 Bushfire Facts	13
5	Moving On - Our Trip Begins	16
6	Townsville	18
7	Camp Five	20
8	1973/74 My Flood Story	24
9	1973/74 Flooding Facts	27
10	Next Trip Begins	30
11	Arriving in Darwin	33
12	Cyclone Season	39

13	1974 Christmas Eve	41
14	The Morning After	47
15	1974 Cyclone Tracy Facts	54
16	2010/11 Queensland Floods	58
17	The Mud Army	62
18	2010/11 Queensland Floods Facts	64
19	Final Thoughts	67

AUTHOR'S NOTE 69
ABOUT THE AUTHOR 70

Preface

What is it really like to live through not just one, but many natural disasters in a lifetime? And why share that story now?

In the lead-up to the Channel Nine special on Cyclone Tracy, aired on Christmas Eve 2024, I wasn't sure I could even watch it. So, I recorded it instead. Then, on the eve of the "50 Years On" commemoration, I found myself in tears as memories I thought were buried came rushing back.

At work, colleagues were talking about it, and when I mentioned I was a Cyclone Tracy survivor, the questions poured in. As I answered, I felt my eyes fill and the tears rolled down my cheeks.

It caught me completely off guard, I hadn't realised how deep those emotions still ran within me. I had to stop, recompose myself, and get on with my day. After all, no one expects to see a woman with red, glassy eyes in the workplace.

Later that same day, while chatting with a customer, I explained how I'd lived through not just Cyclone Tracy but other major disasters too. He listened kindly, then said, *"You should write a book. People would want to read that."* That moment planted the seed.

So, I asked myself: *What do I want to say? How should I say it? And what difference could it make to someone else's life?*

The truth is, I've experienced natural disasters across my 63 years in this beautiful country of ours, my home, Australia. And through it all, my love for this land has only grown stronger. I couldn't imagine living anywhere else.

This is my story, one of survival, resilience, and the power of people coming together.

And so, with those memories stirred and that seed planted, I began to look back on my life and the disasters that shaped it.

Cyclone Tracy destruction on a local Darwin street in 1974
Taken by Karen Feldbauer

Introduction

Surviving Nature's Fury—My Journey Through Fire, Flood and Cyclone isn't just the title of this book it's been the story of my life. Time and again, I've faced cataclysms that tested me in ways I never expected.

I count myself lucky. In my lifetime, I've faced the full force of nature's disasters in many different forms. Each time, I've managed to come out the other side unhurt at least on the outside. The emotional scars, though, took longer to notice.

My story isn't one of devastation or despair from my experiences. Instead, it's about admiration in the way people come together when everything feels uncertain. I've seen complete strangers roll up their sleeves, working side by side like an efficient team. Ordinary people turning into everyday heroes, simply by stepping in and doing what needed to be done.

I'm an emotional person, yes that one who cries at movies, whether it's a tragic family scene or a love story that ends in heartbreak. That side of me means I don't just see events unfold; I feel them deeply. It's helped me understand not only my own reactions, but also the emotions of those around me in times of crisis.

That's what this book is about. It's my journey through some of nature's most powerful moments, told with honesty, humour, and heart. Some of these memories are light and funny, drawn from my younger years. Others I've never shared with anyone before. They're all part of the story; my story, and I'm now finally ready to tell it.

Timeline

1969 January
Victoria bushfire — I was 6 ½ years old.

1973 — 1974 November to March
Queensland flooding on Burdekin River (Camp 5) — I was 11½ years old.

1974 December
Cyclone Tracy — I was 12 ½ years old.

1975 to 2008
Living in Darwin I experienced many other cyclones but nothing like Cyclone Tracy.

2010 — 2011 December to April
Queensland flooding — Volunteered to be part of the mud army cleanup crew.

1

1969 Bushfire

Before the bush fires of 1969 swept through our little corner of Victoria, life in our bush home was simple, adventurous, and full of childhood curiosity.

I was the firstborn of four girls, a winter baby, born in the frosty southern suburbs of Melbourne. My parents moved through a string of temporary houses before Dad finally built our family home on a bush block in the outer suburbs.

To me, the place felt massive though in truth it was just one hectare. Perched on the top of the second hill, our modest three-bedroom home sat high on this long dirt road that turned to dust in summer and mud in winter.

Our block was surrounded by gum trees that lined the driveway and sloped naturally down to the right. The only cleared areas were Dad's big work shed, the front garden, and the roundabout at the end of the drive. Behind the house stood our timber cubby a castle for three little girls with big imaginations.

Our home that Dad built in Research VIC 3095
Taken by Karen Feldbauer

Life there was a mix of adventure and mischief. I discovered nature in all its forms: snails (which, to Mum's horror, I apparently loved to eat), spiders, snakes, the occasional kangaroo, and even the odd horse wandering along the fence line. It was a delightful place to grow up. Mum baked everything from scratch, and I can still remember the sweet aroma of fresh biscuits greeting us after school.

Sometimes, in summer, Mum let us walk the one-kilometre road home from school. To us, that climb up the hill felt gargantuan, and the loose dust or scattered rocks made it easy to slip. But back then it was an adventure. Today, the road is sealed in bitumen neat and tidy, but it's lost that wild edge that made it feel like ours.

From our block, it was possible to cut straight through the bush to Grandma's house. We were never allowed, of course as snakes were too much of a risk. I often dreamed about sneaking off to trek to grans house, just to spite my nagging parents. I've always been adventurous, at ease walking narrow tracks left by wildlife. The bush has always been my happy place.

Mum drove us around in her noisy little black Volkswagen Beetle from the 1950s or 1060s. She loved that car, and I suspect part of it was because the roar of the engine drowned out our constant chatter. Many times, I remember her gunning the motor to get up the wet muddy dirt hill, wheels spinning, car sliding and then when she finally gave up the car slid backwards down the hill. We'd pile out, trudging the last stretch on foot until Dad came home and towed us out with his trusty Land Rover.

That Beetle also left me with a scar. One day at Grandma's house I climbed onto the bumper, slipped, and burned my calf badly on the hot exhaust. Lesson learned, I never did that again, though many, many other lessons were learned along the way.

Example of the VW Beetle that Mum owned
Printed and remastered from a photo off the internet

We always had pets, but living in the bush came with heartbreak. Snakes were ruthless, and many of our animals didn't survive long. I remember a puppy who became sick with distemper. Dad sent us inside; however, me being me, crept out only to see dad put a bullet in this puppy to put it out of misery. Although it was sad and I cried, and screamed at Dad, he explained that the puppy was too sick to survive.

The last dog we had in that house at Research was Simon, our tan scruffy Australian Terrier. He was a tough little dog who followed us girls everywhere. He too, however, became another statistic to a brown snake.

Our Australian Terrier Simon
Taken by Karen Feldbauer

2

1969 My Bushfire Story

Our suburb was next to Kangaroo Ground, and to this day I can hardly believe we survived this bush fire disaster. The blackness left behind in its path of destruction still astounds me. The ground, the trees, the houses, everything reduced to shades of white ash, grey dust, and charred black.

The green bush land I loved had vanished. Even my climbing trees were blackened, crispy to the touch.

On 8 January 1969, I was six and a half years old. That day is etched in my memory as clearly as if it happened yesterday. The heat was unbearable, the air hard to breathe, and the angry black and grey skies bore down on us like a heavy blanket. The wind howled around our house. Even inside, I could feel the heat pressing through the brick walls.

Dad was at work and couldn't get home. He had managed to get a message through: *Stay put. It's not safe to leave by car.* Back then, there were no mobiles, just crackling phone lines and with the power out, we were on our own. My younger sisters and I were huddled in the front bedroom, just as Mum told us to.

Mum had done everything she could to prepare us and our home. The bathtub was full of water. The roof tiles and external brick walls she had been hosing down all morning were wet. Outside the window, through a reddish grey sky that was thick with smoke, I watched her defending our home. A wet towel wrapped around her head and face, a garden hose in her hands, and her colourful 1960's dress flapping in the wind, I watched in awe as she battled to protect us.

From the bedroom floor, I listened to the wind and the sizzling roar of the fire in the trees. The sound grew louder and louder until it seemed the flames were right at our doorstep. The air inside the house was stifling, and still she went out again, patrolling the length of the house, hosing the roof and walls, stamping out embers before they could take hold.

To a child, the fire felt endless. It raged with such ferocity right up to our back door and then, just like that, it was gone. We were alive, not because of luck, but because of one woman's courage. That day, my mother saved us from becoming statistics.

At six years old, I didn't truly grasp what I had witnessed. Only now, decades later, do I understand the enormity of what she did. My relationship with Mum was complex, turbulent and often difficult. Looking back with age and wisdom, I see her for what she was in that moment a one-woman army standing between us and a monster made of fire.

So, to my mother, Faye, wherever you are: thank you. Your bravery did not go unnoticed. You were fierce, determined, and unstoppable that day. You saved your children, and for that I will always be grateful.

Francis Faye Feldbauer — gone but never forgotten.

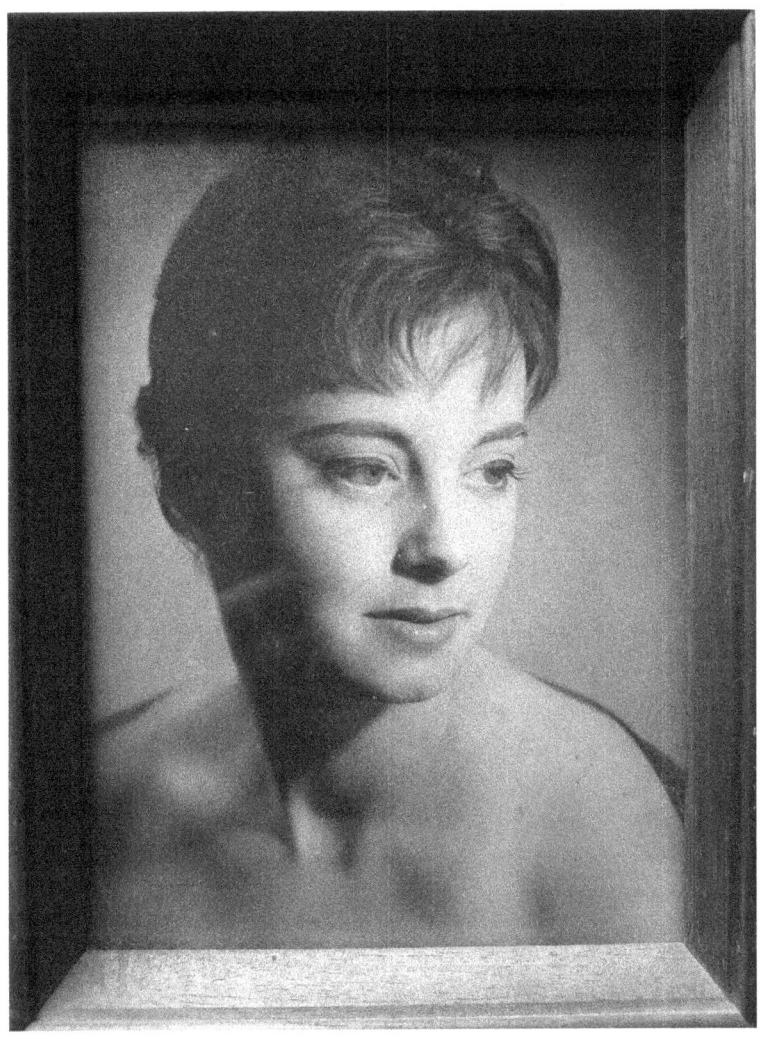

Francis Faye Feldbauer
Photographer Unknown

3

After the Fire

When the fire finally passed, Mum relaxed enough to take us outside and see what was left behind. The air was still heavy, thick with smoke, and hard to breathe. The sky glowed burnt orange in one direction and grey black in the other. Everywhere I looked, there was black, the earth, the trees, even the leaves that remained. They crumbled at a touch, crisp and lifeless. Our front garden was scorched and crunchy underfoot. The green was gone. The lawn was carpeted with ash so much ash.

Hours later, Dad was finally able to come home from work. We all ran to meet him as he stepped out of the car, throwing ourselves into his arms. For the first time that day, Mum cried. The tears came as she melted into Dad's arms, the adrenaline that had carried her through the fire releasing at last. For him, the greatest relief was simple, we were alive.

Mum led Dad around the side of the house where the flames had come closest. Just behind the timber fence stood a lean-to stacked with briquettes and firewood. The raging bush fire had stopped just three metres short of it. The thought of all that fuel catching alight still makes me shiver.

To this day, I believe it was a mix of sheer luck and Mum's extraordinary determination with that garden hose was what saved us from becoming another tragedy of 1969.

Pool for future emergencies
Taken by Karen Feldbauer

Blackened trees 2 year on
Taken by Karen Feldbauer

My memories are personal, but the facts tell a wider truth. To truly understand the impact of the 1969 bush fires, it helps to look at the record of what happened across the state.

4

1969 Bushfire Facts

While my story tells what it was like for one family caught in the path of the flames, the official records reveal the wider truth. At the time, the 1969 bush fires were among the most devastating in Victoria's history, leaving entire communities scarred and forever changed.

The following details are drawn directly from official and historical records. They give context to the day my mother fought for our survival, and they show the scale of destruction faced by so many others across the state.

1969 Bush Fire — The Facts

In 1969, on January 8th, 230 fires broke out in Victoria, burning 324,000 hectares of land. One hectare of which happened to be ours.

Twenty-one of these fires were highly destructive with the worst occurring on the urban fringe of Melbourne. The area's included were Lara, Daylesford, Dulgana, Yea, Darraweit Guim, Kangaroo Flat, and Korongvale. 23 people died in this bush fire.

A fire at Anakie near the Geelong-Ballan Road which had been extinguished the previous day flared up again and moved quickly towards Lara where it destroyed a 90-year-old Gothic church and 40 houses.

Lara bush fires
Sourced from Knowledge AIDR

The worst death toll occurred when a fast-moving grass fire approached the four-lane Melbourne-Geelong Expressway at Lara. Seventeen people died when they left their cars and, in the dense smoke, tried to outrun the fire. Six people who were sheltered in their cars survived.

The event was a catalyst for changing guidelines recommending people are safer staying in a car when the fire is upon them. The fire burnt to the edge of suburban Melbourne affecting Altona, Diamond Valley and Kangaroo Ground. In total 23 people died, 100 were injured, and 230 homes and 21 buildings were destroyed.

> https://knowledge.aidr.org.au/resources/bushfire-lara-and-melbourne-fringe-victoria-1969/

Reading those facts today, I'm reminded that behind every number was a family, a home, and a story just like mine.

5

Moving On - Our Trip Begins

The year after the bush fire, life began to feel normal again. My youngest sister was born, we replanted our garden, and we were better prepared for the future. Our neighbours built their house next door, which meant fewer gum trees surrounding us, and Dad even installed an above-ground swimming pool both for fun and as a potential water resource if it was ever needed. Slowly, the fire became a distant memory.

Dad was a fitter and turner by trade, a handyman in every sense. His Land Rover was his workhorse, but it had no space for us kids. So, one day he built bench seats made from steel frames with timber bases, padded with thick foam and covered in a magenta vinyl. The seats ran along each side of the vehicle, with a little one in the middle, and Dad even fitted seat belts to keep us safe. He also made the bull bar, side rails, a ladder up the back, and a roof rack for our gear and the dinghy. Dad loved to fish.

A few years later, Mum and Dad decided it was time for a change. They sold the house, bought a caravan, and took us girls on an adventure around Australia. At just eight or nine years old, I climbed into that trusty Land Rover, towing our new home, a 22-foot caravan with a purple stripe down the side.

Dad's Decked Out Land Rover
Taken by Karen Feldbauer

Our ginger cat, Cleo, came too, perching herself proudly on the dashboard. Not before doing a morning head count by walking on us all, ensuring we were all present, then she would proceed to sunning herself against the window on the front dashboard.

Saying goodbye to Melbourne, we set off up the east coast. Caravan parks became our homes, filled with new friends and ocean swims. We met people from all walks of life, and soon the rhythms of caravanning life felt natural. Mum and Dad gave each of us a blank notebook to record our adventures, though in truth, I was too busy living them. Even though I did write about my travels in my journal I wish I remembered what I did with it.

6

Townsville

Townsville became an important stop, where Dad found work and we stayed at the Showground Caravan Park (now the Town and Country Caravan Park). School here felt different, the kids seemed taller, older somehow, and I was both shy and curious. But Townsville also brought extraordinary encounters.

One of Dad's jobs connected him with the wild world of motocross stunt riders, including the legendary Dale Buggins and the crew known as "The Dynamo's." At the time, I didn't fully grasp how famous Dale would become, but I loved watching him practice jumps while Dad tinkered with the bikes. He was just a year older than me, kind and approachable, and he even gave me a signed photograph, a treasured keepsake.

Years later, I would learn that at just seventeen, Dale broke Evel Knievel's record by jumping 25 cars on a Yamaha dirt bike in 1978. At the time, though, I simply thought he was the most exciting boy I'd ever met.

Tragically On 18 September 1981, Australian motorcycle stuntman Dale Buggins died in Melbourne. He had built a national and international reputation by the age of 20.

I didn't know it at the time, but I got to know and watch incredible stuntman and woman including Dale's sister Chantell, Spike Cherrie, Max Aspin, Frank Lemon who are all now famous in their chosen fields. I even have their autographs, how privileged am I...

Dale Buggins signed autograph
Supplied by Dale Buggins

7

Camp Five

While in Townsville, Dad got the opportunity to work on the massive project building the railway line from Townsville to Charters Towers as a diesel mechanic. This project was 180 kilometres of train track, with camps one to six set up approximately thirty kilometres apart.

We joined the project at Camp Five which was located on the banks of the Burdekin River. This river was very vast and an excellent fishing spot for Dad.

Camp life was unlike anything I'd ever known. Families filled the fenced compound with their caravans, all working in shifts on installing the new railway line.

With children needing to be schooled we had a little two-room schoolhouse where one teacher taught Years 1–6 and another handled Years 7–12. For me, this was the best schooling experience I'd ever had. Small intimate classes with dedicated teachers, and for the first time I actually felt intelligent and capable.

The camp wasn't without its quirks. Charlie, a massive white-grey bull, had a habit of jumping the grids and wandering through the camp site. He wasn't aggressive but he thought nothing of scratching his itchy belly against a caravan, shaking the whole thing as though an earthquake had struck. You simply got used to it and prayed he didn't put his horns through your caravan walls.

Charlie the bull next to our caravan
Taken by Karen Feldbauer

Nights brought other surprises. Trips to the bathroom required a careful check for green frogs tucked under the toilet seat. Seeing one was fine as long as it didn't jump out mid-pee. Worse still was discovering one when you had to do more than a tinkle. For an eleven-year-old, it was equal parts terrifying and hilarious at the same time.

It was here that I fell in love with green frogs. Tucked inside the bottom of a metal down pipe, they sang their croaky songs, and the echo made it seem as if their voices were bouncing through the air with magic.

Life at Camp Five was full of wonder and freedom. I remember Dad being called one night after heavy rains caused a truck carrying a massive grader to slide off the train track and tip sideways.

He worked late into the night, first securing the machinery, then helping haul it upright, before getting it running again. Watching him handle it all, I felt a mix of pride and admiration.

For me, these years after the fire were a time of rediscovery. From caravan parks to railway camps, I learned resilience, curiosity, and the joy of adventure. The bush fire had taken so much, but it hadn't taken our spirit.

CAMP FIVE — |23|

Truck carrying Grader on its side
Taken by Karen Feldbauer

From bush fires to caravan parks, each step shaped who I was becoming. The next stage of my journey would bring even more change and new challenges I never saw coming.

8

1973/74 My Flood Story

Living on the Burdekin River was perfect for fishing, and Dad loved nothing more than heading out with his mates. I wasn't allowed to go too often, he worried I might tumble out of the dinghy, but when I did, I felt proud to be his little sidekick, his surrogate boy.

I loved helping Dad in other ways too. He'd let me hand him tools while he worked, patiently explaining what each one was for. To me, it was never really about the tools; it was about spending time with my father, Alby. Looking back, I realise those special moments gave me skills I've carried through life, and a fierce belief that no job is "just for men." With all my femininity, I could tackle a task and prove I was capable, however I also know my limits and when to ask for help to get things done.

We celebrated Christmas 1973 watching the Burdekin River rise. I was six months shy of twelve, and my imagination ran wild. I pictured our caravans breaking free and floating downriver like giant tin cans. The real fear, though, was crocodiles; we weren't allowed to go anywhere without adult supervision. As far as you could see, the flooded waters of the Burdekin River were a sight to behold. Although it came close to our camp the water didn't spill over the banks into the camp site as the men had kept us safe.

From November 1973 through February 1974, the floods isolated our camp. The bridge was submerged, cutting us off from the outside world. Food drops came by air. The vastness of water covering the land was unforgettable. The rain never seemed to end, fed by cyclones, Una in December, which became a monsoon trough, and then Wanda in January, drenching the already waterlogged ground.

News coming over the radio spoke of people who were stranded in the middle of these floodwaters. They described the efforts of emergency services and the Australian Airforce conducting evacuations throughout the state which was happening all around us.

For kids, five months felt like forever. Days blurred together with endless rain, sticky nights, and rationed generator power. Each caravan had a timetable for electricity, just long enough to keep food cold. Spam and canned goods replaced Mum's home baking, and we made do. Board games, cards, and invented adventures filled the long days.

Life still carried on. School reopened in its simple form, though heat and power cuts made it patchy. Radio updates continued to connect us to the world beyond our camp. When we could, we'd splash about in the rain or meet friends. The men worked tirelessly to keep equipment safe and operational, while families supported one another with food, medical help, and companionship. Even Charlie the bull stayed with us, calmly grazing and occasionally giving a caravan a good scratch, shaking it like an earthquake.

As a child, I found it restrictive, I felt stuck, just waiting, and always supervised. But I also saw people come together in extraordinary ways. Later, in life, I realised this experience taught me resilience, and how a truly effective team works together for survival.

Flooding is a very different beast to bush fire. The bush fire that nearly took us in 1969 roared through in a matter of hours, hot, stifling, terrifying. Floods creep up slowly, day by day, and linger for weeks or months before the waters recede. Yet they share one truth: everything in their path is changed, flattened, or destroyed.

Once again, we faced the might of nature's fury, and again, we had survived. That choice to survive, to keep going has continued to shape me ever since.

Surviving fire and flood gave me a strength I didn't yet understand. The next chapter of my life would test that strength in new and unexpected ways.

9
1973/74 Flooding Facts

Details as stated on the Bureau of Meteorology website state the following facts about the flooding during this time:

1973 November
Heavy rain, with falls up to 125mm in the 48 hours to 0900 27th, caused flooding in the Paroo, Bulloo, lower Thomson, Diamantina and lower Georgina rivers during the last few days of the month. Major flooding occurred around Quilpie on the Bulloo River.

1973 December
Heavy flood rains during the latter part of the month, resulting from Cyclone "Una", caused major flooding and extensive traffic disabilities in coastal streams between Gladstone and Rockhampton. Moderate to major flooding occurred inland throughout the central and northern reaches of the Fitzroy River catchment and upper reaches of the Burnett River. Flooding also occurred during the month in some far Western and Peninsula rivers.

1974 January

Major widespread flooding occurred in almost all areas of the State during this month. Few areas had no flooding at all. One of these was the Dumaresq River upstream from Goondiwindi, where at one stage during the month, water was released for irrigation.

Record flooding occurred in the Bulloo, Paroo, middle and lower reaches of the Flinders, Norman, Gilbert, Cooper, Diamantina, Georgina and Eyre rivers and creeks as well as Nerang, Brisbane City metropolitan, upper Brisbane, Bremer, Warrill and Logan rivers and creeks, the latter associated with Cyclone "Wanda".

1974 February

As a carryover from the January flood rains, much of the State was still being affected by major flooding as February opened. However, as rain throughout the State eased considerably, flooding likewise gradually eased during the month.

Streams covering the majority of the inland of the State were in major floods. These included Flinders and Gulf, Burdekin, Thomson, Barcoo, Cooper, Diamantina, Georgina, Eyre, Fitzroy, Warrego, Bulloo, Paroo, Condamine and Balonne rivers and creeks. Additional streams in minor flood for a short period were the Tully, Herbert and Burnett rivers.

This situation remained for much of the first two weeks of the month. However, with the general easing of the rain, the river levels gradually receded to the extent that by the 13th, all streams had dropped below moderate flooding. Streams in the far-west were still in flood at the close of the month.

1974 March
During the first week, heavy rains on the Central and North Tropical Coast caused flooding and traffic disabilities. Cyclone "Zoe", during the middle of the month, caused minor flooding in streams in the Moreton region. Towards the end of the month, a renewal of heavy rains on the North Tropical Coast caused flooding and traffic disabilities in the Herbert, Tully and Murray rivers.

Source: http://www.bom.gov.au/qld/flood/fld_history/floodsum_1970.shtml

10

Next Trip Begins

It took nearly five months for the floodwaters to recede before work could restart at Camp Five.

In June 1974, Dad packed us up once again and we set off for the next stage of our journey around Australia. Our teachers gave us schoolwork to take along for the next stage of our trip, though in truth the road was its own kind of education.

Cleo, our ginger cat, resumed her post as family guardian, checking each of us before taking her rightful place on the dashboard between Mum and Dad.

The Land Rover was kitted out with Dad's handmade seats and makeshift seat belts straps bolted beneath the benches. By today's standards unsafe, but to us it felt normal.

Travel brought its own adventures. One roadside stop turned into a comedy when I unknowingly dropped my underpants on an ant nest while going to the toilet. Within seconds of pulling them up I was hopping, stripping, and yelping while my whole family laughed until their sides hurt.

As embarrassing as it was then, it's one of those moments that makes me smile now. Oh, and it's not the only time that I have stripped off my clothes because of damn ants.... But that's a whole other story or two...

We passed through Charters Towers, then at Mount Isa and we stayed long enough to experience my first speedway and rodeo shows.

Fast crazy cars driving around a circular track at high speeds all while crashing into each other seemed silly to me, but it looked like fun.

Cowboys clung to bucking bulls and horses, clowns distracted danger, and I thought the whole thing was madness, however unforgettable madness.

Mt Isa Rodeo
Taken by Karen Feldbauer

Time to hit the road again, what an experience that part of the world was for me and one that would see me venture into speedway racing and rodeo events in the future.

11

Arriving in Darwin

Leaving Mount Isa, we made our way up the Stuart Highway to Darwin, where we settled into the Tropic Trees Caravan Park, directly opposite the local Yarrawonga Zoo on the city's outskirts.

We later learned the park was located at "the 13 Mile," just thirteen miles from the Berrimah lights intersection. Tropic Trees quickly became our new home. We chose a site at the back row of the park, parked our caravan, and began meeting our new neighbours.

Behind the caravan park stretched bush land where we kids often wandered off to play, and Dad would sometimes take us for a thrilling ride on his motorbike. By now, caravan life was second nature to us, so we slipped easily into this new routine.

The park itself was lush and shaded with big mango and other trees perfect for climbing and once again I was surrounded bush land, it was pure haven.

– ARRIVING IN DARWIN

Our caravan in Tropical Trees Caravan Park 1974
Taken by Karen Feldbauer

It was during this time us kids of the caravan park would collect our backpacks, grab some food and head out into the bush lands on our bikes. We would be gone for the entire day and be back before dark; that was the only rule.

We had so much adventure exploring the bush in our backyard; we made bike jumps, followed animal paths and tracks found some sand dunes and climbed some trees. Life was an adventure.

This is something I'll always be so grateful for as I couldn't imagine today's parents letting their children out by themselves in bush land like we did back then.

It was here that Dad's love of fishing and camping in remote, four-wheel-drive-only spots truly began. A passion that gave us the privilege of seeing parts of the Northern Territory that few people ever would get to see. This love of camping continued into my adulthood with like-minded friends and family. The Northern Territory is a spectacular place for camping as long as you knew where to go without the tourists.

The nearby shower and toilet block made daily life easy, and the friendly community soon became like an extended family.

The amenities block nearest to our caravan was built from besser bricks, with two toilets, two showers, and two basins in both the men's and women's sides. Its slightly slanted roof allowed tropical rain to run off, but being in Darwin's climate, there was a wide-open gap between the walls and the roof for airflow. No modern day exhaust fans needed in these showers.

To my delight, green tree frogs often gathered at the amenities block for the water. I adored these frogs, patting them, holding them, and, when my mischievous streak got the better of me, using them to scare others.

One of Dad's English friends, Patrick, was terrified of frogs. With the help of the other kids, I once discovered which shower he was in. I then proceeded to toss a big green frog over the external wall through the gap, and sure enough, poor Patrick screamed in horror. He came bolting out of the shower block, butt naked, yelling at us while we rolled on the grass in uncontrollable laughter.

Of course, I copped the blame and a stern talking-to, but later that night I overheard Dad chuckling about my prank. I was proud of being the only kid brave enough to throw the frog, after all, frogs always land on their feet, just like cats.

Mum and Dad enrolled us at Berrimah Primary School, which meant a 30-minute bus ride each way. At school I was introduced to new tastes. Most memorable were salty plums and green mangoes sprinkled with salt. Salty plums stained my fingers and tongue a bright orange, and I'd gnaw the pip until every last taste of salt was gone.

Green mangoes were eaten in the tree itself. We'd pack a small knife and salt, climb up into the branches, peel the barely ripened fruit, and slice it thin, dusting it with salt before eating. Our biggest challenge wasn't the mangoes but the green ants that called those trees home. While some people considered green ants a delicacy, I had no intention of testing that theory out!

One of our neighbours lived in what seemed to me like a circus tent. It was huge, circular, and held up by a central wooden pole. Inside, the family had everything they needed, from makeshift bedrooms divided by bookshelves to a portable kitchen sink with buckets to collect wastewater. To others it may have seemed primitive, but to me it was ingenious. Each child had their own nook, and the family seemed content and proud of their unusual home.

Living across the road from Yarrawonga Zoo was another highlight. We could visit whenever we wanted, learning about Northern Territory wildlife up close. The zoo had a crocodile named "Gummy," who once appeared in the film *Jedda*, and a buffalo called "Charlie," who later became famous in the *Crocodile Dundee* movie. Yep, in my life, I have met two bulls named Charlie, go figure!

There were enclosures for all sorts of native species, plus a sanctuary for injured and orphaned animals. Visitors could ride the "Yarrawonga Choo-Choo" train around the park to see the animals without suffering in the tropical heat. My favourite resident was the donkey, whose daily "hee-haw" echoed across the caravan park, making us laugh and wince in equal measure. He greeted us this way every day, too and from school.

Living at Tropic Trees Caravan Park in those early Darwin days was more than just a stopover, it was an adventure. Between the bush land play, the frog pranks, the salty snacks, the tent-dwelling neighbours, and the zoo across the road, we were living a childhood most kids could only dream about.

Now-a-days most parents wouldn't dream of letting their children out to play in some of the places like we did as it was such a different time.

It was here that our ginger cat Cleo had her a litter of kittens; she was a cheeky tart who strutted her stuff for attention, this being the end result. We kept my little Boofhead Samuel T. Pyjama Legs Feldbauer "Boof" for short.

Cleo and her kittens (Boof was one of these)
Taken by Karen Feldbauer

12

Cyclone Season

Being new to town, the locals spoke of cyclones as part of Darwin life, so learning more about them became a priority, from the warning signs to being prepared should we ever get to experience one.

Given our home was mobile the caravan park had massive star pickets that were angled in the ground at each site, so dad connected the chains to the undercarriage of our caravan. Our belongings were housed in the annex which included a fridge with top freezer, our bikes, small dining table and chairs for us kids and a few other items.

In early December Cyclone Selma had been predicted to hit Darwin, but it instead tracked north between 1st to 9th December 1974 and passed with no impact to Darwin. Many grew complacent, dismissing warnings about another cyclone "Tracy" that was expected to cross land on Christmas Eve. After all, Selma had veered away. Why would this one be different?

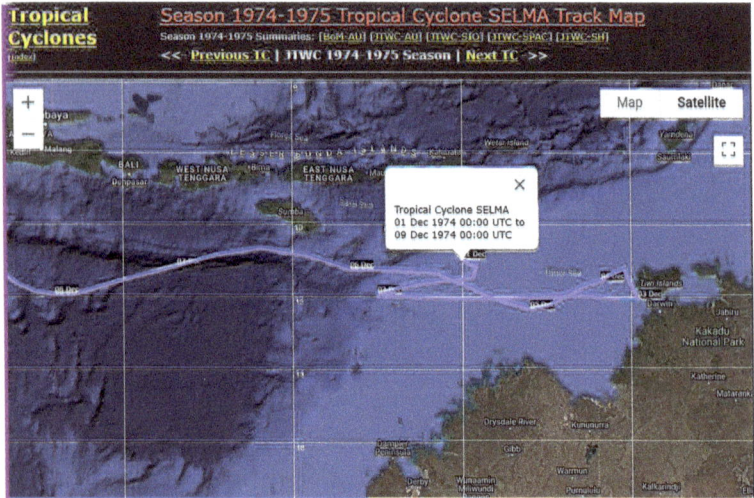

Cyclone Selma Tracking Map
From BOM website

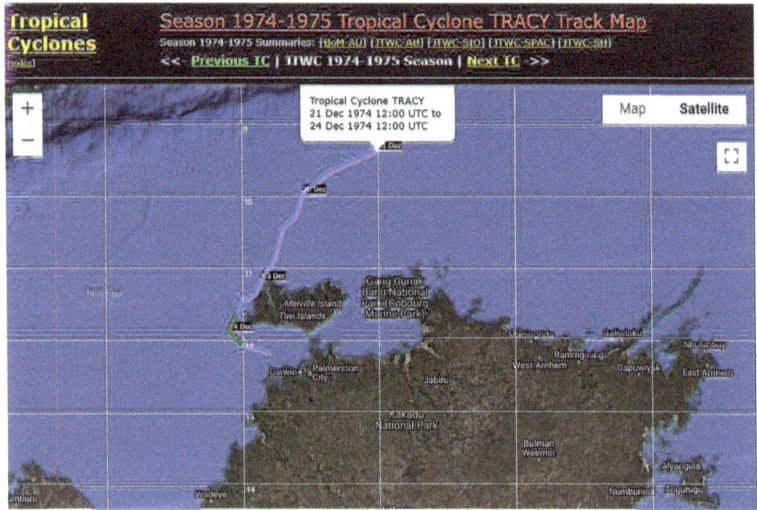

Cyclone Tracy Tracking Map
From BOM website

13

1974 Christmas Eve

That night began quietly. I remember the evening being still and calm with grey skies that looked eerie. At the time I didn't know any better, however I now know it as "***the calm before the storm***".

We ate dinner with friends, and as tradition from Grandma, we opened one gift each, then went to our bunk beds. Outside, Mum and Dad heeded the warnings, helping neighbours pack belongings and dismantle annexes. Dad positioned the Land Rover behind the caravan and secured our bicycles to his bullbar. By midnight, everything was stowed and secured in cars and caravans.

Sleeping on the top bunk bed, I woke to a deafening banging. The howling wind felt like it was all around me. As I lay on my top bunk bed I watched in disbelief as the caravan roof looked like a rolling wave. At one stage I thought the roof was going to cave in on me. It was dark and the only light was coming from a torch that was sitting on the kitchen bench shining upwards to the ceiling.

I was so frightened, trying to think what was happening outside and those horrendous sounds are now etched deep within my subconscious.

Terrified, I leapt from my top bunk to the floor. It was then that I felt the caravan shaking and saw our fridge bouncing despite being tied to a table leg. The wind howled as if the world itself was breaking apart.

Mum, soaked from being outside, rushed in and told me to wake my sisters, get dressed in the clothes on our beds and wait for them. Dressed and ready, while we waited, I picked up the torch and shone it out the kitchen window to see if I could see what was going on outside.

The night felt eerie, it was black and when the lightning would strike, I could make out the trees lashing about as the wind was hurtling them from left to right, front to back. I quickly turned the torch away from the window so as not to scare my siblings. After all I have always been instructed to look after them, that was my responsibility.

My parents came back, tied us all together with a rope around our waists, placed a tarp over our heads and marched us to the toilet block. Looking out from under the blue tarp I could see the lightning. I could hear the roar of the thunder and feel the sting of the thousands of little needles or what I imagined was bee stings. But it was rain hitting our lower bodies with so much force.

Safe in the females amenities block and with a torch in my hands, we were told to just sit and not move. We were all very happy to oblige due to fear of what was happening all around us. This experience was something else and being so scared doing what we were told was not a big deal.

We all huddled together to try and stay dry as the rain was coming in as spray from the top gap between the wall and roof. We shared the bathroom facilities with two other families all huddled in the same shower. At one point during the night, I thought the roof was going to come off the toilet block because of the strong wind but it never did. It was steadfast and rock solid.

You couldn't sleep; you couldn't get comfortable; you couldn't switch off the noise. Even putting your fingers in your ears did nothing to drown out the howling. I was scared as it was relentless however being the oldest sibling I tried to act brave for my sisters and our friends that were with us.

Laying on the concrete shower floor, wet and cold looking up through the gap, occasionally through the lightning flashes I could see the rain and it was still raining sideways. We huddled together and I remember reminding my siblings that we were safe and not to worry as mum and dad were very organised and quite frankly, I was so glad that we weren't in the caravan.

The night seemed to go on forever, so, so long and the relentless howling of the wind was vociferous, so loud.

Many years later as an adult I visited Questacon with my daughter and her gymnastic team in Canberra. While there I visited the Cyclone Tracy exhibit which was a little room setup to replicate what it was like to experience her fiery. I was in total shock as it didn't even register any emotional anguish or even come close to the howling of the winds that I remember, heard and experienced.

I couldn't help myself I just had to tell them that it didn't even come close to the real experience and that if they increased it tenfold it would be closer to the real experience. Not sure if they even listened to me however if you ever get to experience that little room you will understand now that I have mentioned this, and I do believe other cyclone Tracy survivors would say the exact same thing.

Then, suddenly just as quickly as it started, it stopped. It was peaceful, my ears stopped ringing, and you could almost hear a pin drop to the floor. Everything was calm and I thought it was over. It was a surreal feeling, there was no noise at all, it was deathly quiet. You whispered because it was so quiet. The silence, in a strange and macabre way was spooky as if you were expecting something else to happen, like turning around and being face-to-face with a ghost.

The adults went outside to look and while they weren't looking, I peeked out and there were branches broken however everything seemed to be relatively okay. The feeling in the air was eerie, I heard one of the adults mention that the quiet would last for approximately twenty minutes. So, they went to check things out in the park before the storm continued.

They went to see the family in the circus tent, and it was a miracle that it was still standing. They apparently held the tent together with ropes and star pickets. They were exhausted and very wet. The tent canvas was waterproof, though with the wind and sideways rain, it did not prevent water penetrating through the gaps in the walls nor where the sides met the roof. I don't know how they did it, keeping this tent standing, it was astonishing to me.

I learnt later that this was the eye (centre) of the storm. It was now crossing over us and soon it was about to start all over again. This time it would be coming from the opposite direction and was about be more powerful than what we had just experienced. As it changed direction, everything was in reverse.

Twenty minutes passed and right on schedule she started again with more force, strength and louder than the first half of my experience with Cyclone Tracy.

Again, I looked up to the gap between the brick wall and roof. I could see what looked like debris flying. I believed it was the branches from the surrounding trees or bush trees outside the park. At this point I wondered about our cats that were locked inside the caravan.

The rules stated that animals stayed in the caravan. I also wondered about how the zoo animals, were they okay, safe, did they have shelter and what if the crocodile broke out of his containment. So many questions.

In that amenities block, I felt the raw fury of Mother Nature in a way I have never forgotten.

***

Years later I had heard stories of people walking home so drunk on Christmas Eve 1974 not realising what was happening around them. They recall having to lean into the wind while walking against the wind and rain that was stinging their body.

***

As the night dragged on, I clung to the hope that daylight would bring relief. But when Christmas morning finally arrived, it revealed a world I could never have imagined.

14

The Morning After

Christmas morning 1974 felt like it had taken an eternity to arrive. None of us had truly slept; comfort meant huddling in a corner, wishing the noise would stop. My mind was on Boofhead Samuel T. Pyjama Legs Feldbauer "Boof" for short and his mum Cleo. Were they alive and safe in the caravan? Was our home still there?

When daylight finally came, we followed Mum and Dad out of the shower block. The scene before us was surreal. Trees were uprooted, stripped bare, or reduced to debris. Leaves littered the ground like confetti after a battle.

Miraculously, the family in the circus tent had survived, and their tent was still standing; an achievement that defied belief. Exhausted but alive, they had held their fragile home together throughout the night.

My first dash was to the caravan. To my relief, Boof and Cleo were shaken but alive. Dad checked on neighbours, then decided we needed to find his mates in town. With communications down and power gone, the world felt eerily empty. Dad had a strange feeling that we needed to check on everyone that we knew in town, so he took us in mum's car and off we went to find them. What should have been a fifteen-minute trip through Darwin took us more than three hours, weaving through wreckage and blocked streets.

At last, we reached his friend's unit in Alawa. The two-storey brick building was gutted, the roof gone, windows blown out, walls collapsed partly inward however mostly outwards. He found him trapped under his bed; bricks piled across the mattress. Dad quickly took the bricks off the bed and removed the bed from atop of him.

As there was nothing left of his apartment, incredibly crawling under the bed when the bricks fell, was probably what saved his life. Dad pulled him free, and though shaken, he was alive but all his belongings were gone. At the hospital, which was overwhelmed with injured people and running without power, a nurse finally checked him over.

He was finally cleared although later we learned he developed tuberculosis. As we had been in close contact we all had to be immunised. I still dislike needle.

Dad's friends apartment
Taken by Karen Feldbauer

Street of Dad's Friends apartment
Taken by Karen Feldbauer

Driving back home through Darwin, we saw families packing whatever they could and were attempting to leave town. The streets were a mess and without knowing what to do, we went back to the caravan park and waited for advice from the powers to be.

We later learnt that our caravan park was the only one left standing as none of the caravans in our park were damaged.

During this time, we realised that Darwin was in a state of emergency. Back at the caravan park, we waited for instructions. Soon word came that men were to remain, while women and children would be evacuated by air.

Caravan Park destroyed - I believe this was one up the road from us - Bloodwood
Taken by Karen Feldbauer

Not long after the decision was made, we were loaded onto school buses and driven to the airport. There, under a leaking roof in the tropical heat, families waited together. We perched on suitcases, ate sandwiches, played cards, and tried to keep our clothes dry as the rain dripped in. The hours stretched into days.

Finally, our names were called. On the tarmac sat two planes: a Qantas 747 and an RAAF Hercules. I prayed for the jumbo jet, but it wasn't ready. Our group was directed toward the Hercules. Walking up the ramp, I took in the cavernous space, two rows of webbed seats lined the sides of the fuselage while the other two were backed up against each other across the aircraft's centre.

Darwin Airport - many holes everywhere
Taken by Karen Feldbauer

Children sat two per seat, knees knocking against those opposite to each other. Women and children filled the aircraft, belongings secured at the rear. It was loud, rattling, and smelled of oil and metal. But oddly, I felt safe as though the big green and orange machine had wrapped us in its arms. Once we were all comfortably settled the ramp was closed and this massive Hercules started manoeuvring its way along the runway. It was so very, very loud.

The flight was long and bumpy. With no windows to distract us, some kids dozed, others played games, while many including my sister clutched paper bags and vomited from motion sickness.

Hours later we landed in Sydney, only to find that those evacuated on the 747 had arrived well before us. Our ride had been slower, but unforgettable. Few outside the military can say they've flown on a Hercules. From Sydney, we boarded another plane south to Melbourne and the safety of extended family, my grandmother and Uncle Bill (Dad's mum) and Nana and Pop (Mum's parents). The oldest of us two stayed with Gran while Mum and my youngest siblings stayed at Nan's.

Living in the north means learning to expect the wrath of nature every wet season. Over the decades I would face many more cyclones in Darwin, but none ever came close to Tracy. That Christmas morning left an imprint on my heart and mind.

We were lucky. We lost no one, we carried no serious injuries, and our pets survived. But the lesson of that day was seared into me forever: a cyclone is a force not to be underestimated. Everything you love can be taken in an instant if you are not prepared.

For me, it was fear, survival, and relief. For Darwin, it was destruction on a scale Australia had never seen. The facts of Cyclone Tracy tell the rest of the story.

15

1974 Cyclone Tracy Facts

My account is just one family's story of survival. To truly understand the devastation of Christmas 1974, it's important to look at the wider picture. Cyclone Tracy was one of Australia's most destructive natural disasters, leaving a city in ruins and changing countless lives forever.

The following details are drawn directly from government reports and historical records. They reveal the full scale of the destruction the lives lost, the homes destroyed, and the long road to recovery for Darwin.

As an adult I was lucky enough to be employed with a building company which continued in the rebuilding and redevelopment of Darwin.

Evacuation Facts

Approximately 35,362 people were evacuated from Darwin following Cyclone Tracy in December 1974, representing about 75% of the city's population. This was the largest peacetime evacuation in Australian history, with 25,628 people flying south and 9,734 traveling by road to escape the uninhabitable city.

Details of the Evacuation

- Number of people: 35,362

- Percentage of population: About 75% of Darwin's population of approximately 47,000

Methods of evacuation:

- Air: 25,628 people were evacuated by air, including civilian and military aircraft

- Road: 9,734 people left Darwin by road

Timeline

The majority of evacuations took place between December 26 and 31, 1974.

1974 Cyclone Tracy Facts

Cyclone Tracy, which hit Darwin in the small hours of Christmas Day 1974, killed 66 people and devastated 80 per cent of the city.

In the days and weeks following the disaster, most of the traumatised population left the city.

On 28 February 1975 the Whitlam government established the Darwin Reconstruction Commission, which effectively rebuilt the city within three years. Darwin's near complete destruction led to the introduction of improved building codes across Australia.

> Source: Cyclone Tracy | National Museum of Australia

Severe Tropical Cyclone Tracy was a small, but destructive tropical cyclone that devastated the city of Darwin, in the Northern Territory of Australia of December 1974. The small, developing, Easterly storm was originally expected to pass clear of the city, but it turned towards it early on 24 December. After 10:00 p.m. ACST, damage became severe, with wind gusts reaching 217 km/h (117 km; 135 mph) before instruments failed. The anemometer in Darwin Airport control tower had its needle bent in half by the strength of the gusts.

Residents of Darwin were celebrating Christmas, and they did not immediately acknowledge the emergency, partly because they had been alerted to an earlier cyclone (Selma) which passed west of the city, not affecting it in any way. Additionally, news outlets had only a skeleton crew on duty over the holiday.

The fatality count from Tracy was 66 people and the damage it caused was $837 million (1974 AUD, about $7.69 billion in 2022, approximately US$5.2 billion). It destroyed more than 70 percent of Darwin's buildings, including 80 percent of houses. It left more than 25,000 out of the 47,000 inhabitants of the city homeless prior to landfall and required the evacuation of over 30,000 people,[4] of whom many never returned. After the storm passed, the city was rebuilt using more stringent standards "to cyclone code". At the time, Tracy held the record worldwide for the smallest tropical cyclone in terms of gale-force wind diameter, a record that was held for 34 years until it was broken by Tropical Storm Marco in the Atlantic basin of 2008.

Source: Cyclone Tracy - Wikipedia

Behind every statistic was a person, a family, a home and for those of us who lived through Tracy, the memories will never fade.

16

2010/11 Queensland Floods

I never thought I'd experience another major flood again, but in recent years the so-called "100-year floods" or "50-year floods" have become far more common than anyone ever expected.

In 2008 I left Darwin and moved to Queensland. I had the opportunity to live in Hervey Bay, Mackay and then settled in Brisbane. Living in Brisbane often referred to as *The Festival State* thanks to its vibrant arts and cultural scene was a time in my life I grew to love.

I started a business, made lifelong friends, and even reconnected with old schoolmates I hadn't seen in years. Brisbane felt like home for a long while, and I still hope to call it home again one day.

At that time, I worked in the city and commuted daily by train. I'd drive to Wacol station, park the car, and head into work. When the floods began, everyone was on alert. Emergency Services instructed us to be ready to leave the office at short notice.

One afternoon we were told to leave early, and by the time I got back to Wacol the car park had already taken in water.

When I opened the door, I stepped onto wet soggy carpet. That night, instead of putting my feet up, I was pulling out mats and using a water vacuum to try to save the interior carpets of my car. I also learnt that my car had a built in plug for draining any water, how cool was this. It certainly made my job slightly easier.

The news later reported that blocked drains had triggered flash flooding in low-lying areas. Once the drains were cleared, the water receded but it was only the beginning.

These floods brought back old questions for me. How were people coping? How were families keeping safe? How were farmers protecting their livelihoods? The sheer size of the floodwaters, and the length of time it takes for them to recede, can break people down emotionally as well as physically.

2011 Queensland Flooding as waters recede in Wacol
Taken by Karen Feldbauer

When the water finally went down, we visited friends whose homes had been completely inundated. Walking down their street in Oxley wearing gum boots in the slippery mud was heartbreaking: every house in the dips of the land had been flooded, while the ones slightly higher up were untouched.

A stark reminder of poor town planning. Belongings were piled high along the verges. Once-precious items now sodden, broken, and covered in thick, reddish-brown mud. Arriving at our friend's home their garden was gone, and the grass was covered in thick mud that you sank into as you walked up the footpath to the front door.

Inside our friends' home, the muddy water had reached within 10 centimetres off the ceiling. The fridge had floated and bashed its way around the rooms, gouging walls as it went. Wardrobes collapsed into a paper-mâché mess. The only things that survived were her wedding dress and a single wedding-gift a light fitting that they had just installed. Everything else was covered in red mud, damaged and broken.

And then, amid the sadness, a moment that made us laugh as my friend reached into the ruined shoe pouch on the back of her door, a giant huntsman spider leapt onto her shoulder. She screamed; we jumped and then burst out laughing as the poor spider was flung outside. Somehow even that spider had found a way to survive.

Later, we huddled around our devastated friends and reminded them: *yes, you've lost everything you own, but you're alive. You can't be replaced. The rest is just stuff.* After tears, we rolled up our sleeves, respectfully removed the wreckage, and cleared the mud so the insurance assessors could see the damage.

This process was happening everywhere and as far as we could see. At the end of the day we all went home very muddy, exhausted but grateful for being able to help and thankful that we were okay.

The overwhelming need to clean up homes and businesses across the devastating 2011 Queensland floods that were now covered in thick, smelly sludge is what brought about the need for volunteers which was called The Mud Army.

17

The Mud Army

In 2011, Brisbane witnessed something extraordinary; the emergence of the "Mud Army." Thousands of volunteers armed with gloves, shovels, and sheer determination turned out to help strangers. I was one of those who put their hands up to volunteer. Having been through a flood already, I felt compelled to help the wider community however I could and this was my way of participating.

We were bussed out to affected areas and went door to door, asking families how we could help. This incredible display of community spirit and resilience helped many residents recover from the disaster.

I'll never forget one woman breaking down over a cheap pedestal fan. Someone had said, "It's just a fan, it can be replaced." But in that moment, it wasn't about the fan. It was about memories, stories, and attachments woven into all her belongings. That fan was the final straw for this woman. We reported back to the group leader and help soon arrived to assist her with her anguish.

Helping her made me reflect deeply. Our things are more than "stuff." They hold meaning, connections, and reminders of who we are and where we've been.

It took me back to a small memory from my childhood; two circular leather coasters I once carved with horse heads. I stained one red, the other blue. I accidentally left them in my school desk, and they vanished. That was over fifty-five years ago, but I still feel their absence.

Those coasters mattered to me in a way no one else would ever fully understand. They were my creation, something that I designed and made using the skills I had learnt from my teachers. These were the beginnings of my creativity and later I gained a Diploma in Graphic Design Foundation.

So why do we place so much meaning on our belongings, knowing they could be lost in an instant? Maybe it's because they anchor us. Maybe it's because they hold our stories. And maybe, just maybe, it's because they remind us of who we are.

After all, *everything is replaceable... or is it?*

For me, it was about mud, loss, resilience, and survival. For Queensland, it was a disaster that touched nearly every community and the official record tells the bigger story.

18

2010/11 Queensland Floods Facts

My story is just one small part of what happened during those months of relentless rain. To understand the true impact, we need to step back and look at the bigger picture.

The 2010–2011 Queensland floods were among the most widespread natural disasters in Australia's history.

What began as weeks of heavy rainfall quickly escalated into an emergency that affected towns, farms, cities, and industries right across the state.

The following information is drawn from government reports and historical records.

These facts show not only the scale of destruction, but also the extraordinary response of communities and volunteers who came together in the face of crisis.

2010-2011 Queensland Floods — The Facts
Quick Statistics

- 33 Fatalities
- $2.38 billion Insurance Costs
- 3600 Homes Destroyed
- 3572 Businesses Destroyed

In late November 2010, rain began falling in Queensland. By January 2011, extensive flooding had impacted 75 per cent of the state and a disaster zone was declared. In total, 33 people lost their lives, with three bodies never recovered and declared deceased by the State Coroner in June 2012. Evacuations numbers totalled 5,900 people from 3,600 homes. An estimated 28 000 homes were in need of rebuilding; scores more would require extensive repairs. The final report of a judicial inquiry into the event was published in March 2012.

The economic and commercial impact of the floods was significant. Approximately 3,572 businesses were inundated, with an estimated $4 billion in losses across the mining, agriculture and tourism sectors. Nineteen thousand kilometres of road were damaged, and three major ports significantly affected. Over 28 per cent of the Queensland rail network was left twisted and displaced.

The Insurance Council of Australia estimates the 2011 damage at $2.38 billion.

Affected Areas

On 25 December 2010, Cyclone Tasha crossed the northern Queensland coast and brought disaster to every river system south of the Tropic of Capricorn, and as far west as Longreach and Charleville. The flooding engulfed Alpha, Jericho, Chinchilla, Dalby, Theodore, Warwick, Bundaberg, Gayndah, Munduberra, Emerald, Rockhampton, Condamine and St George. The Condamine River, the Balonne River, the Burnett River, the Comet River, the Dawson River and the Nagoa River reached flood peaks never before recorded.

On 10 January 2011, a wall of water swept through Toowoomba, then travelled west, flooding Oakey, Dalby, Chinchilla and Condamine for a second time. This caused flooding through the Lockyer Valley, including Murphy's Creek, Postman's Ridge, Helidon, Grantham, Laidley, Lowood, Fernvale and Forrest Hill.

The floodwaters affected the Bremer, Lockyer and Brisbane River systems, reaching heights that engulfed Ipswich, Goodna, Gailes, Karalee and suburbs of Brisbane.

> https://knowledge.aidr.org.au/resources/flood-queensland-2010-2011/

The official record explains what happened. My final thoughts are about what it all means the lessons I've carried, and the resilience nature has taught me.

19

Final Thoughts

After Cyclone Tracy, some dear friends from Melbourne who were living in Adelaide at the time jokingly told us not to move there because "disasters seem to follow you." We laughed, but in truth Adelaide is Australia's most earthquake-prone capital city.

It is located on several fault lines, including the Para Fault and the Eden-Burnside Fault, which run through or under its northern, eastern, and southern suburbs. With tremors of magnitude five or six occurring often enough to be a real concern. So, while I've visited Adelaide many times and enjoyed its charm, I will never make it my home.

Even though my family left Melbourne to travel via caravan around Australia we ended up coming back to Darwin when allowed during the rebuild and established ourselves in what became our new home. Living in Darwin during that period of regeneration was both exciting and unsettling. Everyone wondered: *when will the next big cyclone hit?* Yet in the 50 years since, no storm has matched Tracy's fury.

Many lessons were learned, and as someone who later worked in the construction industry, I know firsthand that Darwin's building codes became some of the strongest in the nation often making other states' standards look inadequate.

Although I left Darwin in 2008, it will always be my home. Still, I believe that "home" is ultimately where your heart is. It is with deep gratitude that I share these life experiences of surviving different natural disasters.

I hope they are seen not through a negative lens, but as stories of resilience, humanity, and the shaping of the person I have become.

I like to think of myself as caring, kind, and patient person, always willing to lend a hand when needed. After all, isn't that what humanity is truly about?

Writing this book has given me space to reflect, to honour those moments of fear and courage, and to find meaning in the challenges nature placed in my path. This is only a small glimpse into a life shaped by the power of the natural world, but I hope you find it as rewarding to read as I have found it to write.

Until next time... *bon voyage.*

Karen Feldbauer (Kazbar, Kaz)

Author's Note

This book is not just about disasters, it's about people, emotions, and the unexpected strength we find when life changes in an instant. I've written it, not only to share my journey, but also in the hope that others who have lived through tough times might see themselves in these pages.

Some of the memories you'll read here have never been spoken of before. They are my truths, shaped by fear, resilience, and the surprising light that can shine even in dark times. If my story brings comfort, reflection, or even just a smile, then writing it has been worthwhile.

ABOUT THE AUTHOR

Karen Feldbauer is a storyteller, adventurer, and survivor. Having experienced multiple natural disasters across Australia, she brings a unique and deeply personal perspective to resilience, community, and the human spirit. Through her writing, Karen hopes to inspire readers to see strength in their own journeys and to cherish the bonds that hold us together when life feels uncertain.

SURVIVING NATURE'S FURY

KAREN L FELDBAUER

www.ingramcontent.com/pod-product-compliance
Lightning Source LLC
Chambersburg PA
CBHW061731070526
44583CB00024B/3088